Mountaineering

Anthony Dover

To Dad

Gran

There's snow on those mountains
 Said my grandmother
 Whilst I was eating
 A bowl of weetabix

Later we watched
Crown Court
And I became aware
Of good and evil

In the evening
We went to the park
To play cricket
Three boys older than me
Asked to have the bat and balls
So they could play
My Grandmother immediately
Saw them off
And said
Don't be so trusting of people.

The Sandman

For what is a grain
Of sand
But the remnants
Of a mountain

All matter comes from this
Sand
Dreams
Who keeps your hopes up
During the night
But the Sandman.

The 10 year writer and painter

Trapped in the poverty trap
He went on
All the time
Walking
All the time
Thinking

And then as everyday
Like concourse
He walked quite literally
He walked
Up a hill
 And his friends said
 Came down a mountain

Soon he reached into
 His unconscious
 And pulled out
 A 30 year old with potential

Only when he has
Written all he can
And painted until
Will his life be
Over.

The Dream King

Between the pedestal of Night and Morning
Between red death and radiant desire
With not one sound of triumph or of warning
Stands the great sentry on the Bridge of Fire
o transient soul thy thought with dreams adorning
Cast down the laurel and unstring the lyre
The wheels of time turning turning turning
The slow stream channels deep and doth not tire
Gods on their bridge above
Whispering lies and love
Shall mock your passage down the sunless river
Which rolling as it seems
Shall take you king of dreams
Unthroned and unapproachable for ever
To where the kings who dreamed of old
Whiten in habitation monumental cold.

James Elroy Flecker 1884-1915

Illusion

If there is a roof to the world
Surely it is jealously guarded
By a roofmaster
Who prevents the
Lid coming off
This tiny world.

It's an illusion
The children cry
How they cry
When they've
Seen other worlds.

Surely the children
Keep bad at bay
When the only word
They've left to say
Is
Dream.

Three friends

If each reality
Is a person
How indebted my father
To the three peaks
 In the Peak District.

Penygent
Great Whernside
Ingleborough

 Three great policemen
 Detectives too
  Aiding him in his quest
 In his quest
 For justice
 And peace.

The Shamen

Have you ever
Taken peyote
In silent darkness
This is a test
For all truth.

Native indians
The spirit that
Moves as one
Through the world
They call alcohol
Firewater

I can move
Any mountain
Flinging them
Into the ocean
No more misery
No more infinity

Blackout blackout
It doesn't exist
Disillusionment
Means
See through everything
Dream life.

The Enigma of Kaspar Hauser

A mountain
The world population
Struggling up
Deaths peak.

They keep dragging
Them down.
Life is the answer
No
Its an addiction

I have desires that are never met
And most of my life was spent
Education.

He professed his faith
Fell down again
Finally knifed
By superstition
A legacy of negative
Life.

Old one

No time
No age
A cave.

Immense good
Released from his
Death.

How cruel Cahadras
How bereft
His people.

There's not enough
God to go round.

Peaks and Troughs

Mt Arafat
Kilimanjiro
Sugarloaf
Olympus.

Mat my coat
Killing me on benefits
Don't forget the sugar and bread
Hope you've got your camera.

It's a world event.

St Elmo's Fire

The faces have changed
Since you were
Young

No more beauty
No more hope
My generation was
Coming alive.

Nearly a rebellion
Few survived
The sad contemplation
Dead on arrival.

The ice pick on the
Founders
Glowed blue
St Elmo was on fire.

Diggy takes his pick
Smaugs lonely mountaineer
Speak friend
And enter
The guest of winter.

Spring

Of the mountain king
 Appelation Spring

 There's plenty of
 Molehills to go
 Round
 To be climbed
 The Chimes

 What do you
Dream at the top
 It deludes and dehabilitates
 The son of God.

Because it is there

Money was invented
To save a dying society.

Play your part
The art

The grains of the cross.

They reincarnate souls
To make money

Which is real
The paintings of the price.

What a price to pay
For fish

So sorry
I was turned away

Raining cats and dogs
She climbed me

To get to the top
Not St.Elmo's fire
Jacob's ladder
Would have done.

Big Ben

Stop the clock
Stop the clock
Scotland
Nevis
Lost.

Evolution
Exhibition
Existence
Stop

The Loire valley
The Pyrenees
Fire to start
These.

Top of the world
Innocence
One Way out
Mustn't forget
Cezanne Mt San Victoire
Vincent.

The Subcontinent

The passage to India
 Christianities boum
The toe ring on
His daughters room

 Perfect Charas
  To get there soon
  So many places
  So soon.

  Himalayas
 So subject
  I doubt
  I'm really here

   Before you disappear
   Utter east
   It has been.

    I'll put on my clothes
    The vending machine
    For the noticed moment
     We'll meet again.

Marco Polo

The trail to the East
Centuries ago
The Spice road
A sight.

How could he travel
Alone in a caravan
 The Rockpools
Minituare
Mountains
 The sandcastles
 Keep

Bullets

A train so fast
You leave your souls behind
 Mt Fuji
Rewind
Cruel to be kind.

The Northern range
The blue veins
 Like spreading the news
 Gurus.

 Angel
 Feeling her dreaming
 Nodes.

The truth
 Escaped the gun
 Hallucination
 Carl Jung

 We know now
 Kennedy was won
 A girl killed him
 One so young.

Quietitude

Mountaineering
A quiet religion
In the shadow of
The Quimsy mountains
The Vale of hope

Blue mountain
Blue mountain
A vision of America
Pthalo blue
And each poem
Of the picture.

Humous the hobbits
To a lesser God
Lembas
Passed round
With quick

The quiet earth
If he hadn't
Suicide
A moment before
A moment after.

Tidy

If you are messy
A messiah you are
If you are dropping hints
'On Everest

They'll talk you into
Being God
 A hard job
 What a fate a responsibility
When all you did was drop rubbish
 Keep Britain Tidy.

The Rift

The rift valley
A corridoor
In blessed Africa
 The North Atlantic Ridge
 Squeezing out mountains

 When America was laid by
 England
 Its historic means met.

 Pyrenees in Spain
 Fire in the dark
 Usually Urals
 Harden his heart.

 The Dream Thief came
 On Mars we conquer
 Its future its paths
 Its mountain ranges
 Photographed.

Between a rock and a hard place

The Rockies
San Fransisco
Still Grinding
 The shelf
 Who knows when
 The big one
 Will come
 To itself.

 The Andes
 A hard place
 Here he found a future indeed
 With his new wife
 To run from the place
  The rock and the sun

Rite of passage

Snowdon
You could have been
One
Running up the Welsh mountain
Nothing on his feet.

An Indian raffia
LSD trip
So clear to behold
Divine creation
foretold.

Reaching the top
Last certain if you will
Primal Scream my will
I was a God.

You here strange stories
Behind the bar
The crowded climb
Off the presses
What is time
So many now
So few survived..

Mt. Zion

As I climbed Holy Mount Zion
The last one.

I thought how
Poor a thing
To only have mountains
For friends.

 Mt Zion was
 The bravest the few
 Saw Gesthemane different
 A zenith of truths.

 The knowing hologram
  Chiba's children grew up
 Artificial intelligence found out
 Each mountain was a chip
 An electronic relationship.